LOOK AND FIND®

SHREK 2 ™

Illustrated by Art Mawhinney

Published by
Louis Weber, C.E.O.
Publications International, Ltd.
7373 North Cicero Avenue
Lincolnwood, Illinois 60712

www.pilbooks.com

Manufactured in U.S.A.

8 7 6 5 4 3 2 1

ISBN 1-4127-0472-3

 publications international, ltd.

There is much celebrating in the swamp! Shrek and Fiona are married! Everyone has gathered to see them off as they depart for the kingdom of Far Far Away. Can you find Shrek and Fiona and some of their friends at the bon voyage party?

Donkey

Fiona and Shrek

Gingerbread Man

3 Bears

Wolf

3 Blind Mice

Magic Mirror

Everyone in the kingdom of Far Far Away has been waiting for Fiona to return home with her handsome prince, especially the members of the Official Fiona Fan Club. Look for them in the crowd.

"I'm Fiona's biggest fan!"

"No, I am!"

"Who said I'm not Fiona's biggest fan?"

"Where's Fiona?"

"I am Fiona!"

"I want to be Fiona!"

"Fiona rocks!"

The King goes to the Poison Apple to get some help with his little ogre problem, but he gets more than he bargained for. One bad apple spoils the bunch, and this is the bunch! Can you find these bad seeds in the crowd?

Tweedledee and Tweedledum

Little Bo-Peep

Little Red Riding Hood

Simple Simon and the Pie Man

Rip Van Winkle

Georgie Porgie

Wee Willie Winkie

Shrek went to the Potion Factory to ask Fairy Godmother for her help, but she refused. If Shrek wants to be handsome, he is just going to have to take matters into his own hands. As he makes his way toward the Potion Containment Room, can you find the effects of these other potions that are not so well contained?

Sleepy-Time

Frog Lotion

Lamp Polish

Beauty Balm

Small Aerosol

Golden Eggs

It's business as usual in the kingdom of Far Far Away, but that doesn't mean that it isn't unusual business. Can you find these uncommon things on the busy street?

TurboCoach XL7

Lord and Tailor bag

designer quiver

Big Bad Woof

vanity plate

FFA 1

The A List

ironed suit

The fairy-tale creatures are gathered at Shrek's hut to watch the ball coverage, but behold! Knights are in pursuit of some very bad boys, and everyone is amazed to find out that the bad boys are Shrek and Donkey! Find these other amazing items in Shrek's hut.

heights

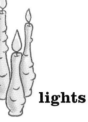

lights

bites

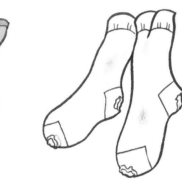

delights

whites

tights

frights

When this rescue mission is complete, Shrek and Fiona will want to thank all the little people who helped make it possible. Look for the little people storming the castle.

Little Bo-Peep

Little Boy Blue

Little Miss Muffet

Thumbelina

Itsy Bitsy Spider

Little Red Hen

Wee Willie Winkie

Chicken Little

Shrek's rescue mission to save Fiona from Prince Charming's kiss has not gone according to plan. It is better than planned! With Fairy Godmother out of the way, everything is back to normal. Find everything as it should be.

The Little Mermaid

Cinderella

Peter Pan

3 Little Kittens

Rapunzel

The King

Pinocchio

Go back to the swamp and find these things that will help Shrek and Fiona on their long journey.

___ suitcases

___ map

___ picnic basket

___ spare tire

___ banner

___ road sign

___ bread crumbs

___ rainbow

Go back to the red carpet and look for these Far Far Away stars who are disguised in the crowd.

___ Beauty and the Beast

___ Little Boy Blue

___ Cinderella

___ Rapunzel

___ Aladdin

___ Mary and a lamb

___ Peter Pan

Go back to the Poison Apple and find these famous Jacks who are down on their luck.

___ Little Jack Horner

___ Jack and Jill

___ Jack B. Nimble

___ Jack Sprat

___ Jack of Hearts

___ Jack and the Beanstalk

Go back to the Potion Factory and look for some of Fairy Godmother's favorite snacks.

___ french fries

___ soft tacos

___ Renaissance wrap

___ strawberry ice cream

___ glazed donut

___ ham and cheese sandwich

___ pretzel

___ pepperoni pizza

Go back to the busy street scene and find these things.

___ 31 pairs of sunglasses

___ 15 hand mirrors

___ 15 double skim cappuccinos, no foam, no sugar

___ 5 off-duty limo drivers

___ 3 mother and daughter duos

___ 1 child star

Go back to Shrek's hut and look for these delicious onion snacks made in his honor.

___ onion dip

___ onion rings

___ bag o' onions

___ purple onions

___ pearl onions

___ green onions

___ onion blossom

Mongo wasn't the only secret weapon the fairy-tale creatures cooked up. Go back to the castle gate and find these things from the Muffin Man's kitchen.

___ eggbeater

___ wire whisk

___ measuring spoons

___ oven mitts

___ dinner fork

___ rolling pin

___ frying pan

Don't walk away yet! Go back to the ball and find this fun and fancy footwear.

___ flipper slippers

___ glass slipper

___ ballet slippers

___ bunny slippers

___ Shrek's slippers

___ fuzzy slippers